# "We Refuse to be Anyone's Enemy"

# The Story of the Tent of Nations, Palestine

## by Daoud Nassar

ISBN: 9798852478054

# DEDICATION

To my wife, Jihan, and to my wider family, without whom this book could not have been written, and without whose support and encouragement our story would be very different from the one described in the pages that follow.

# CONTENTS

Chapters                                                          Page

1   A plot of land                                               1

2   My immediate family                                          8

3   My younger years                                             14

4   The legal battle                                             17

5   Intimidation                                                 27

6   Isolation                                                    30

7   Palestinian reaction                                         34

8   My father's hopes, and the circumstances that               38
    influenced them

9   Planting a tree and making a difference                      53

10  Learning from Christ                                         56

11  Our vision                                                   59

# 1 A PLOT OF LAND

I was driving the tractor on our farm.  Suddenly my way was blocked by a young man with an M16 rifle slung over his shoulder. "What are you doing on our land?" he demanded.  "It is not your land;" I replied, "it is ours, and we have the deeds to prove it." "You may have all the papers; but God gave us this land; that is why it is ours and not yours."

So, our story is connected with land, and land is the core issue in our struggle.  Our story here on this land, which is called Daher's Vineyard, and more recently The Tent of Nations, started in 1916, over 100 years ago.  And it has been more than a century of struggle to keep the land.

My grandfather bought this land in 1916, during the Ottoman occupation of this part of the world.  It is a hill-top farm near the Palestinian village of Nahalin, a few kilometres south-west of Bethlehem in what is now the West Bank, or occupied Palestine. Two good things he did after buying the land are important for us now.

The first thing is that he registered the property with the Ottoman authorities.  At that time, many landowners deliberately failed to register their land in order to avoid having to pay property tax. Sometimes if they had bought, say, 100 dunam [1], they might register one dunam so as only to pay tax on the dunam registered. This failure to register was to have disastrous consequences for the descendants of the original owners in our present situation under the Israeli occupation. But my grandfather carried out the necessary registration in the correct way: he registered all the land, and paid taxes on all the land. Moreover, he registered the property under the name of his youngest son, Bishara (my father). That he did this has turned out to be a great blessing to us as far as establishing our title to the property is concerned, because we have not had to go back beyond my own father's generation.

Part of our hill-top farm showing an Israeli settlement across the valley on the neighbouring hill

The Ottoman Empire collapsed at the end of the First World War and, when the British occupied Palestine under the Mandate given by the League of Nations, they carried out a new registration of land. We re-registered, and again when the Jordanians occupied the West Bank during the first Arab - Israeli war of 1948. By that time this land was in the ownership of my father and my uncle, and the re-registration on each occasion was quite straightforward because all our papers were in order. This was the situation until 1967, when the Israelis occupied the whole of the West Bank and refused to allow any Palestinian to register land.

The second good thing my grandfather did was that, after buying this land, he and his family left Bethlehem where they had all been living and began living on the farm. The first home for my grandfather's family on this land was a cave. At that time, it was not unusual for Palestinians to live in caves, caves that are scattered in profusion all over this part of the world. Caves are warm in winter and cool in summer, and are easily protected. Caves can be made into very acceptable homes. Some of the houses in the old city of Bethlehem are built on to the mouths of caves. The caves themselves can be used either for storage or as a shelter for the livestock belonging to the family.

This move from Bethlehem to this hilltop farm was a big decision for my grandfather. He sold his house and abandoned the style of life he had been used to in the town of Bethlehem. To this cave he brought his wife, Adibe -- my grandmother -- and their three children. My father was called Bishara, which means 'good news'. He was the youngest, and his two elder brothers were Naif and Sleeman. The three children were between five and twelve years old when the family left Bethlehem. Although caves can be made comfortable homes, it wasn't the easiest thing for my father and his two brothers to grow up living in a cave. They really did have to begin a completely new way of living here on this farm. But my grandfather wanted to encourage in his three sons a real love of this place. More than that, I believe that from the first moment that he set his eyes on this land, he had a vision for it that we as a family have inherited.

I am convinced that my grandfather was a deeply spiritual man. In the evenings he would gather the family together around the fire for prayers and hymn-singing; there was an almost biblical atmosphere about the place. So my father and his brothers were brought up in an atmosphere of spiritual sensitivity. My father became something of an evangelist in his own right in Bethlehem, spending some of his free time leading prayer meetings there and working with children and youth in the town.

You see, my father was born during the Ottoman occupation of this country and died during the British occupation. My understanding is that these occupations deeply affected his thinking, and had a major impact on his hopes for this farm, which he often spoke about with his children. His vision was somehow to create on this hill-top farm a place where freedom, justice and peace-making would thrive.

When my grandfather and his family moved to this hilltop, the soil had never been worked. It was in its original barren state: there was nothing here at all, except earth and rocks; there are always plenty of rocks in Palestine! Slowly but surely, my grandfather turned this land into a farm. He worked, together with his growing sons, on cultivating this land. He planted olive trees, and also a great many vines from which he began making his own wine, wine that he was able to export to different places in Europe.

My grandfather died a year or two after he had bought this piece of land and settled his family here. I think he may have died of a broken heart. This is how it happened. His second son, Sleeman, suffered an accident on the farm when he was about 12 years old. I am not sure of the exact circumstances, but I think he may well have been bitten by a scorpion during the harvest season. Whatever it was, my father rode off on his horse to summon a doctor from Bethlehem. By the time he had returned with the doctor it was too late; Sleeman was dead. I know that my grandfather blamed himself for his son's death, and he died about six months later, while he was still a relatively young man.

After my grandfather's death, the farm became the responsibility of my uncle, Naif, and my father and, of course, my grandmother. It was a big challenge for my grandmother to continue to cultivate the farm with, now, no husband and only two of her three sons, both of them still relatively young at the time. However, they all rose to the challenge and the farm continued to thrive.

My father set up his own accommodation in another cave on the farm.  He was now into his 40s, and he had not married, and indeed had no plans to marry.  He had committed himself to looking after the farm with his brother, and to carry forward his own father's vision.  However, he met a young girl (who was to become my mother) when she came with her mother to a Bible class that my father was leading in Beit Jala, near to Bethlehem.  She was only 15 years old at that time.  So you can say that my mother and my father met 'in church'.  Although many marriages in Palestine are still arranged between the parents of the bride and the parents of the groom, my mother and father met, fell in love, and married one another.  That was quite unusual for the time.  It was a huge change for my mother: leaving her home in Beit Jala and coming to live on the farm in a cave !  But she gladly made the change, and is still alive, still living on our farm.  She, with my father and my uncle, looked after my aged grandmother, and she was soon bringing up a family of her own.  We did have a property in Bethlehem to which the family would go from time to time, but my mother also became very committed to the land.

Then another tragedy struck.  During the Arab rebellion of 1936 [2] we lost a great many of our vines, and to this day we do not know who it was that uprooted these bushes.  Was it the British; or the Jews; or indeed some of our own people?  All I do know is that our farm was in a troubled area during this rebellion against the British.  The Arabs had become convinced that the British were favouring the Jews.  Jewish immigration was increasing rapidly and upsetting the delicate balance between Jew and Arab, with the Jews becoming increasingly powerful and acquisitive of land.  It was during that time this farm was badly damaged -- we still have copies of the claim for damage that my father and my uncle submitted to the British authorities at the time.

So, twenty years after my grandfather began the cultivation of this land, my father and his surviving brother, with their mother, had to rebuild the farm and replant.

Twelve years later brings us to the first Arab/Israeli War of 1948 that began as soon as the British left and the Jews here declared an Israeli State. The Jews call this war their War of Independence; we Palestinians call it Nakba, the Catastrophe. Until then, for all the difficulties and problems from time to time, many Jews and Arabs had been living together in this country side by side, for the most part getting on reasonably well together in one, undivided land.

The 1948 war brought its own difficulties. This farm and the neighbouring village of Nahalin are very near to what became the 1949 Armistice Line (known now as the Green Line) between Israel and Palestine. My father and his brother faced a number of difficulties, even though the farm was not inside Israeli territory. There was, for instance, a huge refugee problem in the area, which resulted in three refugee camps being established on the outskirts of Bethlehem. These camps, with scores of others, are still in existence over seventy years later. But, the fact is that all these troubles and difficulties that my father's generation faced did not disconnect my family from the land my grandfather had bought. My family have lived here continuously; the land has been worked continuously.

It was sometime during the 1950s that my grandmother became ill. My father took her to hospital in Bethlehem. For some while he was travelling back and forth between the farm and the hospital to visit my grandmother. His brother continued to live in the family cave, while my father found another cave on the property, and this became his new home. He continued to live there until his death in 1987.

*Notes:*

[1] A dunam is 1000 square metres, or about a quarter of an acre.

[2] The 1936–1939 Arab revolt in Palestine was a nationalist uprising by Arabs in Mandate Palestine against British colonial rule and mass Jewish immigration.  The revolt consisted of two distinct phases. The first phase was focused mainly around strikes and other forms of political protest. By October 1936 this phase had been defeated. The second phase, which began late in 1937, was a violent and peasant-led resistance movement that increasingly targeted British forces. This rebellion was brutally suppressed by the British Army and the Palestine Police Force, using repressive measures that were intended to intimidate the Arab population and undermine popular support for the revolt.

# 2 MY IMMEDIATE FAMILY

I have already written briefly about my father's marriage to my mother. His bride was called Milade, and her family originally came from Jaffa. They were refugees, driven out of Jaffa by the Israelis in 1948. The family sought refuge in a village near to Ramallah, a town about fifteen kilometres north of Jerusalem. Later they moved from there to Beit Jala (near Bethlehem).

My grandfather and grandmother with their children and grandchildren

Living on the farm was far from luxurious, even if my father's cave was quite comfortable. No wonder he had not seriously contemplated marriage as a younger man, since he did not think that his way of life would be very attractive to a woman.

However, love overcomes all kinds of obstacles, and my mother and my father set up home happily in this cave.

Their first child was Mary; she is now married and living in Jerusalem. Then came Daher, my oldest brother; he and his wife still live on the farm and he and I work the land. After him was George; George was married in 1991, and he and his wife lived here on the farm until the beginning of the second intifada. One of their three daughters has a heart problem, and they found that she could receive the kind of treatment she needed at a hospital in Virginia in the United States; so that is where they are now living. Georgette is my parents' next child. She is married and living in Australia, and she keeps telling me that I am foolish to stay here doing what I am doing when I could so easily find a much happier and easier life for both myself and my family in Australia! She is very persuasive, but I'm still not persuaded! Next comes my sister Amal who works as a physiotherapist in the Caritas Baby Hospital in Bethlehem. Nahida followed her; she is married with five children and is a kindergarten teacher in Bethlehem. Then there is my sister Najwa; she is married, also with five children, and living with her family in Jordan. I am next in line! I am married to Jihan, and we have a daughter called Shadin who is twenty-five, another daughter Nardine who is twenty-two, and a nineteen year old son whose name is Bishara, named after my father. Bishara means 'good news', and he was born on 20th September, which we Christians keep as Holy Cross Day, so we also gave Bishara another name, Stavros, which is a Greek word for 'the cross'. My understanding is that the good news is always connected with the Cross. Two years younger than me, and the last of the children, is Tony, born in 1972.

My father died on what is known as 'Land Day' [4], on 30 March 1976. He left my mother with nine children, five daughters and four sons. The oldest was 22 years old at the time; I was five years old, and Tony was three. By this time we were living in a house in Bethlehem during term time, so that we children could go to school.  But at week-ends and during the school holidays we were always back at the farm, living there and tending the land.

My elder brother Daher with his wife, Katy

My wife Jihan and me

Jihan's family have emigrated to the United States.  Jihan trained in computer science in the United States, and teaches in schools here in Bethlehem.  Like me, she is very committed to the farm and all that we are trying to achieve here, and of course also to our local village of Nahalin.  At the community centre there Jihan gives a great deal of time to encouraging the young women of the village to learn new skills such as a knowledge of English and how to use a computer.  Like many Palestinian villages, Nahalin is socially a very conservative one, and the young women of the village tend to lead somewhat restricted lives.  My wife is keen to help them broaden their horizons without undermining the accepted social conventions.

Let me tell you how we came to choose the name Nardine for our second daughter.  Nardine was born in 2002 while Israeli forces were invading Bethlehem during the second intifada [3]. Our Bethlehem house is near the Church of the Holy Nativity, and the Israeli army had encircled the church. For forty days we were under siege, and life was very difficult, particularly for Jihan, carrying Nardine at that time. In the weeks before her birth, in June of that year, I was in fact away from home on a speaking tour in Germany. When I arrived back in Jordan [5], I was not able to return to Bethlehem by any direct route, because the roads were blocked by soldiers. Every Palestinian city was isolated from other Palestinian cities. In order to return home, after I reached Jericho, I had to walk through the desert and on minor roads, avoiding all the checkpoints, picking up taxis where I could. Nardine was born while I was making this journey. We had not chosen a name for her, not least because my wife and I were apart at the time of her birth. Now, my tortuous journey back to Bethlehem took me through the town of Bethany. What came into my mind as I made my way through this town was the biblical story of the anointing of Jesus by Mary in the house of Lazarus. It was to be Jesus' final visit to Jerusalem, just before his arrest and trial, and he was staying (as he often did) with some of his disciples at the house of Lazarus, and Mary and Martha his sisters. During supper, Mary took some costly oil and poured it over the feet of Jesus as he reclined at table. Judas protested at the waste, but Jesus said that her action would always be remembered and that she had done this "in anticipation of my burial". He already knew he had not long to live. So I thought to myself, Why not give her the name Nardine which, in Arabic, means 'a costly oil'? The old English word is 'nard'. When I arrived home, I suggested to Jihan that we should call our newly born Nardine, and explained why. She was delighted.

There was a tradition in this part of the world that when a daughter of the family was married, her parents would give her a necklace on which was suspended a tiny vial of alabaster containing some very costly scented oil. It was a way of her parents saying to their daughter, "You are now leaving us to live

11

with your new husband; but you will always be very precious to us." It may well have been this tiny vial of oil that Mary broke open and poured over the feet of Jesus, saying to him by doing that, "I fear that you may be taken away from us, but you will always be very precious to me."

The journey back to Bethlehem was a difficult one, not to say a dangerous one. At any stage I could have been arrested for breaking the curfew. But, with the help of many others, I was able to make the journey successfully and arrived at the village of Beit Sahour near to Bethlehem. From there I walked to my home, sheltering in the houses of friends when I felt it was unsafe to use the roads. Looking back on this journey, it was full of one frustration after another, and at times I asked myself why I, and other Palestinians, had to suffer in this way. But, good came out of it because, without making the journey, I would not have passed through the town of Bethany, and would not have thought of calling our daughter Nardine. St Paul once wrote that all things work together for good for those who love God, and I really have come to believe those words regarding the troubles that we have experienced.

Because of the very restricted lives that we Palestinians have under the Israeli occupation, some may wonder how I get permission to travel overseas. My visits overseas are not regarded as 'political' by the authorities. I confine my talks to telling the story about my family and about our land and, yes, about my struggle to keep it from being taken from us. Getting the necessary visas and permits to travel overseas is not always easy, and sometimes I have to wait quite a long time. But so far I have not been refused.

*Notes:*

*[3] Intifada literally means 'shaking off', and describes a Palestinian uprising against the Israeli occupation of the West Bank and Gaza Strip.*

The second intifada began in September 2000 and resulted in the death of over 5000 Palestinians and over 1000 Israelis.

[4] March 30 is an annual day of commemoration for Palestinians of the events of that date in 1976. In response to the Israeli government's announcement of a plan to expropriate thousands of dunams of land for 'security and settlement purposes', a general strike and marches were organized in Arab towns from the Galilee to the Negev. In the ensuing confrontations with the Israeli army and police, six Arab citizens were killed, about one hundred were wounded, and hundreds of others arrested.

[5] West Bank Palestinians are technically 'stateless' and can only enter and leave the West Bank through Jordan, if they can obtain the necessary travel documents. Israelis and people from other countries pass through Ben Gurion Airport near Tel Aviv.

# 3 MY YOUNGER YEARS

My father gave me the name of Daoud, or David in English, and my mother tells me that I was one of his favourites. Not only was my father a devout Christian, but also he absorbed into his own thinking his father's hopes for this land. He died when I was only five, and I found it rather difficult to grow up as a boy without knowing a great deal about my father. Most boys in my class at school had both parents alive. They would talk about some of the enjoyable things that they did with their father, and the gifts their father gave them and so on, and inevitably I felt rather different and left out. I also missed very much not knowing my own grand-parents. But my mother is a very strong woman, and she has devoted her life to her children and to the farm, and so my brothers and sisters and I grew up in a loving home and with a great love of this farm.

I finished my secondary schooling in 1988, and I wanted very much to go on to study at a university. Although all of us completed secondary school, no one from our family had yet been to university, not least because we needed to work on the farm to support the family. However, good fortune came my way. I was a member of a Bible study group, and in 1989 the pastor offered to arrange for me to go to Austria to study at a Bible School for six months. I accepted the offer immediately, although of course I knew not one word of German.

So off to Austria I went. I worked for a time as a volunteer in order to learn the language, and then started my studies at the

Bible School.  At the end of my studies, I was due to return to Palestine, but this was during the first intifada (1987-1989) and all the Palestinian schools and colleges were closed.  So I decided to remain in Austria, and I was able to find a university in Linz that taught computer science and was prepared to offer me a place.  However my high school certificate was not recognised in Austria, so I went back to school there in order to study for a qualification which would allow me begin my computer science course.

I very much enjoyed my studies at the Bible School, and although I have always been interested in theology, so far I have felt that the role of a pastor is not for me.  I am already fully committed in other ways, not least in helping to look after the land my grandfather bought.  Also, the fact that I am not a pastor does not mean that I cannot be involved in Christian work such as leading Bible studies and in work with young people.

The problem regarding my university course was that my studies prevented me from doing any paid work, and I did not have a scholarship to support me while I was studying.  So quite soon the money ran out and I was faced with a big decision: whether somehow to find some money and stay in Austria and complete my course, or return to Palestine.  The more I thought about it, the more I realised that I just had to return to Palestine, although what I really wanted to do was to stay in Austria.  I had already been two and a half years in that country and was very quickly adapting to a new way of life.  I now spoke German quite well; I enjoyed the kinds of freedom that were denied to me as a Palestinian in my own land and, when I had taken vacations from study back in Palestine, I was already feeling something of a stranger among my own people.  However, In late August 1991 I set off back for Palestine, feeling that there must be a good reason for my return, but not knowing at that stage what it was.  I was soon to discover!  But, for the moment, it was back to my studies.  A month after my return, I started a course of study at Bethlehem University in business and major accounting.  After completing my B.A. degree, I began working in the field of what we call in Palestine 'alternative tourism', and I also received a scholarship to study in Germany.

My sister Amal

My mother, who still lives on the farm

# 4 THE LEGAL BATTLE

However, in October 1991, two months after my return to Palestine, the government of Israel declared our farm as 'state land' [6]. And I saw the hand of God in my reluctant decision to return from Austria. Because from that moment my family and I began a new chapter – a chapter that is still incomplete -- in our struggle to keep our land, and to farm it and use it as my grandfather and father intended. The legal battle to retain our land had begun.

The Israeli authorities have adopted a number of different strategies in an attempt to deprive us of our land.

- The first strategy is to make it as difficult as possible for us to prove that we were, and are, the legal owners of this land. And this is what this chapter is about.
- The second strategy, with at least the connivance of the State, is harassment and intimidation , mostly by 'settlers', as they are called, from the new Israeli towns by which we are surrounded.
- The third strategy is of isolation.
- Then there have been offers of cash, very large amounts of cash, to persuade us to relinquish ownership of this farm.
- Lastly, there is the whole exhausting business of having to go from 'pillar to post' to get a just decision about our ownership of this farm, and being met with constant postponements and new demands, not simply month after month but year after year. The Israeli authorities hope that we shall come to the point of despair and just give up,

"throw in the towel", as they say.

If you find that these next few paragraphs are exhausting to read, just think of how exhausting it has been to have to live through this whole rigmarole, which is still incomplete!

We did not hear about this move against our farm, declaring it as 'state land', from the authorities; we met some friends who told us that they saw a number of soldiers and other military personnel, and Jewish settlers, on our land, and these friends were wondering what had happened.  The fact is that many Palestinians who have owned a plot of land for ages do not have the proper registration papers.  In a particular village it will be well known that a certain family owns a particular plot of land, but that is not good enough for the Israelis who use the lack of proper paperwork as an excuse to designate such land as 'state land'.

My family's farm is located in an area that the Israelis have designated as a settlement [7] area called Gosh Etzion.  This is one of the settlement blocs that the Israelis would like to keep in any future peace agreement between Israel and Palestine.  There are now three major settlement blocs in the West Bank: this one at Gosh Etzion; the Maale Adumim bloc to the east, and another bloc to the north called  Ariel.  The Israelis are attempting to establish a permanent presence in these three areas by taking over these parts of our homeland for Jewish settlements and adjoining farms.

Once a plot of Palestinian land has been declared 'state land' by the authorities, the burden falls upon the owner of the land to prove his ownership.  An appeal against the declaration of 'state land' has to be made to the court within 45 days.  We are the only family in this area who has appealed against such a declaration, because most of the families have not had the necessary papers through which to prove ownership sufficient to convince an Israeli court, even though it is well known locally that they are indeed the owners. Our family was fortunate to have a grandfather who properly registered our land and paid taxes on it, and we have all the papers to prove this.

My brother Daher went to the Absentee Property Office in Bethlehem and there showed the officer [8] all our registration papers. The officer was very surprised, and somewhat annoyed. "Where did you get all these papers from?", he asked. The next step was to go before a military court to plead our case. We went with our lawyer, who presented our papers to the military judge. The judge was rather taken aback to see such a complete set of papers, and he immediately postponed the case. This is the usual tactic when a judge is shown overwhelming evidence of Palestinian ownership: he is reluctant to find in favour of the Palestinian, but cannot find in favour of the Israeli state without appearing totally unjust and unreasonable; so he simply postpones the case.

We would be told, "Yes, these may be genuine papers, but we don't think that they necessarily refer to your particular land. These papers look as if they might be referring to an area in Bethlehem and not to your farm near the village of Nahalin." One reason the court suggested this was because they recognised us as a Christian family, and asserted that no Christians owned land in or near this Palestinian village. In fact, we were not the only Christians who had owned land in this area; others had done so in the past, but they had sold their land to Muslim Palestinians.

Within this strategy of casting the onus of proof upon us, their next ploy was to say to us that the land survey included in our papers was not accurate and up-to-date, because it was drawn up in 1922. We were given 35 days within which to produce an up-to-date survey. And for the court to recognise this survey, it would need to be counter-signed by all our neighbours, indicating their agreement with the boundaries as shown on the new survey. It was very difficult indeed to obtain all the necessary signatures. In the first place, at the time when my grandfather first purchased the land, we had just four immediate neighbours. Since that time the properties bordering on our land had been subdivided several times. To establish accurately who were all the present owners of the land surrounding our property was far from straightforward. And when we had done so, to persuade some of these people to sign a very official and important looking document was also not at all easy. "What are we being asked to sign, and why? The whole village knows that the land on this survey is your land, and has been as far as back as we can remember. Perhaps if we sign, it will alter the entitlement to our own land in some way, and prejudice us." I'm sure you can understand why some of our neighbours were reluctant to add their signature to this new survey.

We worked day and night, and within the 35 days obtained all the signatures that were needed. How we managed it, I still do not know; but we did! In the end, everyone who was asked to did put their signature to the new survey. But when we brought our new documents to the court, again our case was postponed. The usual ploy!

The court next asked us to produce eyewitnesses; that is, people who could personally testify that the land in question was indeed our farm; that they had seen us working it, planting olive trees and so on. We managed to assemble about 50 of our friends and neighbours who were prepared to testify, and we brought them with us to court on the appointed day, that is to the military court near Ramallah. We were kept waiting outside the court in the sun for nearly 5 hours, after which a soldier came out to tell us that the court had no time to deal with our case on that particular day, and that we were to return tomorrow with our witnesses. It is not difficult to understand the reason for this postponement: the court was no doubt confident that we would not be able to produce so strong a group of witnesses on the following day, particularly as we, and those we had assembled, had been kept waiting so long during the day when our case should have been heard. No doubt the judge was looking forward to being able to write across our papers, "No witnesses; case closed."

However, we managed to persuade all those who had gathered on the first day to testify to come again on the following day. When my mother eventually went into the witness box, she was questioned for a very long time, perhaps two hours. Here was an elderly lady being cross-questioned by a military judge about every detail of her life. Of course, the judge was speaking in Hebrew, and his questions were interpreted into Arabic. From time to time our lawyer, who spoke both Arabic and Hebrew, would intervene, explaining that the interpretation of either the question by the judge or the answer by a witness was not accurate.

Time and again, when the date of a hearing was due, we heard either on that very morning or the day before that the hearing had again been postponed. As I have said, postponement is a tactic used by the courts to avoid having to give a decision unfavourable to the Israeli state. There have been numerous occasions when we have consulted with our lawyer to prepare the best possible case for our next hearing, trying to imagine what questions we will be asked and what evidence we will have to produce, only to be told at the last moment that the case has been yet again postponed.

In the year 2000, that was during the second intifada, our lawyer received a brief fax message from the court telling him that our family had not produced sufficient proof of ownership of the land, and therefore it was going to be taken over by the Israeli state. The fax also said that the family had 40 days in which to appeal against this decision to the Supreme Court. And this was said to us without, in all these years, having had the opportunity of a full hearing before the military court due to the repeated postponements.

These years of legal battle before the military court had been expensive enough.  How on earth were we going to able to find the money needed to bring the case before the Supreme Court?  Our lawyer was very understanding, and agreed to postpone the payment of his fees until we could find the money.  But going before the Supreme Court meant that we had to engage a different lawyer, because a lawyer from the West Bank cannot appear before this Court in Jerusalem.  This had to be a new case with a new lawyer.  We managed to find a Jewish lawyer who would take a case.  He made it absolutely clear to us right from the start that to plead our case before the Supreme Court would be very expensive.  He asked for $10,000 as a down payment!  From friends and family we managed to raise the sum of money, and the lawyer began to build up a new case, and lodged our appeal to the Supreme Court within the 40 day time limit.

So in 2002, a new legal battle started in front of the Supreme Court.  One of the first things the judges of the Supreme Court said to us was that those who carried out the land survey required by the military court were not recognised by the Supreme Court, and that a new survey would be necessary.  This task would have to be carried out by Israeli land surveyors.  These surveyors would also need to go to Istanbul so that they could check all the original registration papers, placed there by my grandfather.  They would also need to check back on the registration required by the British during the time of their Mandate.  The cost of this new survey was about $70,000.

After the hearing of our case by the Supreme Court had been postponed a number of times, in 2007 the Court decided to refer the case back to the military court.  Clearly, the Supreme Court had realised what a strong case we had, but were reluctant to decide in favour of us and against the State of Israel.  To do so might have established a precedent to which other Palestinians in similar situations could appeal. Instead, the Supreme Court recommended to the military court that a solution to this dispute should be found by agreement between the parties outside of a court hearing.

Following this referral back to the military court, that court sent a fax both to the Supreme Court and to our lawyer stating that the court had no objection to our family registering our land in the Israeli Land Registry. By that statement, the military court does recognise us as owners of the land. However, the court demanded that we should re-register the land so that it could recognised as private property within Area C of the West Bank under total Israeli control. But our land had already been properly registered, and we had produced all the papers to prove this. Why, we thought, did there need to be this re-registration? It became clear that the requirement for this re-registration was yet another ploy to put us to a great deal of extra trouble and extra expense, in addition to all the time and money we had already spent. For this re-registration, we would have to prepare yet again a new survey, collect again the signatures of our neighbours and so on. This we did, and we presented the papers, only to be told after a couple of postponements that we had not presented enough documents.

The reader, I am sure, will understand that all these postponements, referrals from one court to another, demands for new surveys and further documentation and the hiring of lawyers became a very costly business, and so far we have spent in the region something like $270,000 seeking to establish the ownership of our land. These costs have been met largely by generous individual donations, often from people who have become Friends of the Tent of Nations in Europe and in the United States, and from church congregations, to whom my family and I am most grateful.

We were ready to 'go again' by 2013, only to be told by the Israeli authorities that they had lost our file! This saga begins to sound more and more like 'Alice in Wonderland'.

The whole process was started for the third time, or was it a fourth?, in 2015, and in 2019 we were told by the court that the documents we had presented were satisfactory, the land had been properly surveyed and all the fees had been paid. What was now required was a visit to the farm by the New Registrations Committee, so they could check that the boundaries on the land coincided with the boundaries as shown in the survey. At the end of their visit to the farm we were informed that they had been unable to identify some of the boundary markers on the land, and that a new land survey would have to be undertaken.

And so, yes, we undertook yet another survey .... our farm must be the most thoroughly surveyed piece of real estate on the whole of this planet!

The Committee revisited the farm in July 2020, and on that occasion we gathered our neighbours would also be able to vouch for our ownership of that piece of land. We were told that the Committee would be meeting again in February 2021 and that we would then be informed of the next steps that we would need to take. The Committee duly met, but without informing our lawyer of the outcome, and in September of the same year our lawyer informed the Committee that if he had not heard from them by the end of the month he would take the whole matter back to the Supreme Court. We were informed that we would hear of their decision on 13th December but, surprise surprise!, this was postponed to January 2022, then May, then October. The Committee did, however, actually meet in November. We later discovered that the reason for these postponements was that the State Custodian for Land had failed to appear at any of the earlier meetings. A good way of postponing a perhaps unacceptable outcome is simply not to turn up when decisions need to be made!

The Committee summoned all the objectors to attend this November meeting. There were seven objectors including, of course, the State of Israel, also some local Palestinian neighbours who, between them, had issues about a right of way over our property and the positioning of a boundary fence. In addition there was one particular objecting family from the neighbouring village of Nahalin who have been for some years been extremely hostile to us and the plans for our farm, and about whom I will mention more in the next chapter.

This hostile family did not attend this November meeting, in spite of being summoned, and were dismissed from the case. The Committee then decided that they would meet again on 16 January 2023 and, going against their own rules, re-invited the hostile family to attend. Between this November and this January date we went to see all the objectors except this family and were able to sort out with each one of them the particular problems they had, and in each case came to a solution that was satisfactory to the objector.

At the January meeting, we presented these solutions to the Committee, and it was agreed by all that these particular objectors should withdraw. Also, the State Custodian for Land failed to appear yet again, which was of great embarrassment to the Committee, and he was dismissed from the case. This dismissal was, of course, to our great advantage. Some other very significant people did come hoping to attend this meeting, including members of United States Embassy and representatives from several European Missions in Israel. All were denied entry on the pretext that the meetings of this Committee were not open to any members of the public.

Without reaching any final decision, further postponements took place in both February and May. As I write these words in June 2023, we await the next meeting scheduled for 6th September 2023. And all this can be described in two obvious words 'constant postponement', no doubt hoping to exhaust us and drain our spirits.  But that won't happen: there is a lovely Palestinian word 'sumud'; it means 'steadfastness'.  We are in for the long haul, however long it takes.


*Notes:*

*[6] There are a number of Israeli laws the purpose of which is to acquire for the state as much land as possible previously held by Palestinians. The laws are complex, and some derive from Ottoman occupation and British Mandate days (where that suits the Israelis' purpose).  For example, if it can be shown that a plot of agricultural land has not been cultivated for three years, it becomes state land.  Yet there are now many farmers who cannot access their land because of the separation barrier and limited access through checkpoints.  The same applies if ownership has not been properly registered.*

*[7] 'Settlement' is a misnomer, suggesting temporary dwellings.  Israeli settlements in the West Bank are new towns with all the modern conveniences such as swimming pools and the like.*

*[8] All Palestinians in the occupied territories live under military law, and their cases are heard in military courts.*

# 5 INTIMIDATION

The date is Friday, 28 January 2022; the time is around midday. It is cold and there is snow on the ground. I am working in an underground garage on our farm fixing a tractor – underground, because we are not allowed to erect any kind of building above ground. My brother Daher is feeding the animals nearby. I stop what I am doing because I suddenly hear Daher shouting. Then I hear him clearly bellowing "I shall call the police." I turn to leave the garage to see what is going on and am confronted by a group of men, one of whom hurls a large stone at me which I am able to avoid. I run from the garage with these attackers in hot pursuit, who catch up with me and start to beat me with metal rods and sticks. The same thing is happening to my brother.

Clearly, this attack was carefully planned, but – fortunately for us – not carefully enough. This group of about twelve men came at the time when they were convinced that my brother and I were alone on the farm. They were all masked and all wearing the same kind of overall to prevent any kind of identification. And they were all carrying powerful weapons to wound and perhaps to kill.

But, by the mercies of God, there were in fact two others on the property, my wife Jihan and a young woman from abroad who had joined us to work on the farm for a few weeks. This young person had been preparing lunch, and came from the kitchen to call my brother and me to tell us that the meal was ready. She saw what was happening but, before she could act in any way, someone among the group of attackers shouted, "There is an international here, and she has seen us." At that alert the whole group stopped their attack and fled from the farm. Daher and I were left severely injured, bleeding and bruised, but we were alive!

Daher managed to get up come to where I was lying to see if he could help. I said to him that I was O.K, at which point he fell to the ground and lay unconscious for about twenty minutes. Surprisingly, I was able to get up and run to fetch my car without feeling any pain at all – that came later – to take Daher to hospital. But Jihan had called an ambulance and the police, and we were soon driven away to hospital.

We still do not know who all this group of attackers were, except that they were Palestinians almost certainly from the nearby village of Nahalin, and that among them were the four members of this family who have been attacking our farm in various ways – cutting down olive trees and vines and setting fire to some of our orchards – for some years prior to this incident. Whether they have been doing this on their own initiative or because they have been encouraged and paid by others we simply do not know.

This attack was certainly the most brutal we have suffered, but intimidation is not a new experience for us.

So, we have come to the second strategy, that of intimidation.

Jewish settlers from nearby settlements (illegal in international law) have on several occasions attacked this farm. They have come and uprooted our trees, damaged our water cisterns, and threatened us with guns. Three times they have tried to build a road across our property.

This kind of harassment, which is very widespread in the West Bank against Palestinian farmers, is designed to persuade us to abandon our land and leave.  In whatever way they can, they want to make life as difficult as possible for us.  On one occasion, in 2002, when they attempted to build a road across our property, we managed to obtain a court injunction against them.  This made the settlers very angry, and to punish us they uprooted about 250 of our olive trees.  We managed to replant these trees with money given us by a Jewish organisation called European Jews for a Just Peace in Palestine.  Not only did this organisation give us the money, but members from it came to our farm and did the planting with us.

# 6 ISOLATION

The third strategy is that of isolation. Our farm is now surrounded by five Israeli settlements. It is the only piece of property in this immediate area under Palestinian ownership. We are about 950 metres above sea level, with a very pleasant view to the west. On a clear day we can see right across this land to the Mediterranean Sea. It is the kind of location that is particularly coveted by the Israelis. Right across the West Bank, it is on the hill-tops that most Jewish settlements have been built since the West Bank was occupied in 1967. These settlements dominate the high ground not only visually, but also in terms of military strategy.

If the Israelis could take over our piece of land, they would then dominate this area totally, completely encircling the Palestinian village of Nahalin in the valley below us. But we are staying put, not least as the last hope for the 7500 people who live in this Palestinian village. And the time may well come, quite soon, when we will have to live permanently on the farm, because the Separation Barrier that is still being built could cut us off completely from Bethlehem.

The Separation Barrier, the official reason for which was to protect Israel from Palestinian communities on the West Bank, in fact encroaches into the West Bank very significantly, and now often divides a Palestinian village from the neighbouring Palestinian village. The Barrier has little or anything to do with security, but is simply a strategy for stealing as much Palestinian land as possible, and again making life as difficult as possible for

Palestinian communities. In some places this Separation Barrier still only exists on paper and has not actually yet been built, many years after it was started.

Because of our fear that this Barrier, when complete, may mean that Bethlehem, our nearest town, may be much more difficult or impossible to access than at present, one of our chief objectives is to make the farm as self-sufficient as possible in every way that we can: self-sufficient in water collected in cisterns; self-sufficient in electricity from solar power, self-sufficient in biogas by installing the necessary converters of food waste and compost into flammable gas; and self-sufficient financially in terms of what the farm can earn by what it grows. In this last objective we have experienced significant setbacks because of attacks on our farm and the uprooting of a large number of olives and vines and other trees. As I write we had hoped to harvest twelve to fifteen tons of grapes to produce both Chardonnay and Cabernet Sauvignon wines for the market. But a recent destruction of many of our vines and other fruit trees has made this impossible and, not for the first time, we have to start all over again. Our philosophy is always to hope for the best but also be realistic enough to prepare for the worst.

It is part of Israeli policy to isolate Palestinians living in villages and rural areas so as to make life so difficult for them that they will leave their homes and move into the Palestinian towns, if not out of the country completely. By this means the Israelis will be able to create urban Palestinian ghettos easy to control while the rest of the West Bank will be open for them to live in and use as their own country.

Quite apart from what the Separation Barrier has in store for us when complete, the authorities have attempted to isolate us in a number of ways. Anyone coming to this farm discovers that the road to it has been blocked by the Israeli army in two places with large boulders and rubble, and the road itself has been damaged.

The road to our farm, on the hill-top beyond, blocked by the Israeli authorities

This farm is in what is known as Area C, under complete Israeli control (something that was intended to be a purely temporary measure under the Oslo Accords). One effect of the Israeli control is that we have been denied all access to water and electricity. The water that we have is now all collected in rainwater cisterns around our farm; the electricity we have is generated by solar panels, generously given to us by a German organisation, and stored in batteries. We are also denied all permits to build on and improve our farm.

So, the authorities are doing everything they can to prevent us developing the farm, even agriculturally. Also, a number of bypass roads are being built that directly link all the settlements, but these are not open for Palestinians to use. We have to use roundabout secondary roads that are often in poor condition and journeys take a great deal longer.

Our water is
collected in rain-
water cisterns,
and our electric-
ity is generated
by solar panels

In May 2010 we were served with nine demolition orders, regarding structures that we had erected without a permit. Among these are tent frames and shelters for the animals. We are not talking about substantial stone structures, but temporary frames to give shelter to our guests and volunteers, and for our animals. I said to the officer who served me with these demolition orders, "Even according to Israeli law, there are some settlement outposts around here that have been illegally erected. If you are going to serve me with demolition orders for putting up structures without a permit, why don't you serve the same kind of orders on those illegal settlers?" He told me that this was none of my business.

# 7 PALESTINIAN REACTION

I do want to emphasise that our own story is in no way unique. This kind of thing is happening to Palestinians all over the occupied territories. This provocation is forcing many Palestinians to respond in one of three ways: by violence; by resignation; or by departure.

There are some people in Palestinian society who believe that through violent retaliation we could achieve some of our just objectives. I do not think this is possible, nor do I think that it is right because I do not believe that in the end anything worthwhile is achieved by visiting violence with violence. Any violence on our part, as you know, is met with violence by the Israeli authorities out of all proportion to any violence Palestinians use. The State of Israel has very sophisticated weapons and a highly trained army; we mostly have sticks and stones, and yes, I am sad to say, the occasional suicide bomber and crude rockets fired from Gaza. I completely deplore suicide bombing and the use of rockets, but it is not difficult to see why these means of retaliation are sometimes used. And, of course, our re-acting in a violent way to the persecution we suffer is quite pleasing to the Israeli authorities, because it gives them a reason for their continual complaint that all of us Palestinians are terrorists, bent on their destruction. It gives them a good reason not to seek a genuine peace with us, and to maintain the present war status and the occupation. Indeed, I believe that for the Jews to make a genuine peace with us Palestinians would be inconvenient to the Israeli government, because then it would have to treat us with respect and as equals rather than as a people to be contained, oppressed, and if possible removed.

There are other Palestinians who say that we must wait until the international community can bring about a just peace, a peace that we Palestinians and Israelis have not been able, between us, to achieve. These folk are resigned to their fate until others come along to help them. They are waiting until the Americans and the European Community put sufficient pressure on the Israelis to establish a just peace in this land. Of course, this will necessarily also involve the Palestinian leadership, which at present is weak and divided. I see no immediate prospect of the Americans changing their unconditional support for the State of Israel, and little hope of the European Union taking an independent and just approach to our present plight. So, for the foreseeable future the Israelis will continue to hold most of the cards in the pack. And the fact of the matter is that a peace process was started as long ago as 1991 (the Oslo Accords) since when our situation has deteriorated significantly. The Israeli bulldozer remains pointed in exactly the same direction and is moving steadily forward.

A third group among us have no confidence in either what violence would achieve or what the international community has the will to deliver, and this group, comprising mainly of the best educated within our community, are simply leaving the country. Among them are many who are Christian, because in general terms the Christian community is the better educated. In 1946 Christians in what is now Israel/Palestine represented about 30% of the population; now we are less than 2% ...in Jesus' native land! I have already said that one of my sisters is living in Australia. Every time I speak to her on the telephone she tells me that I am foolish to continue to live where I am: there is a much better life waiting for me in her new country, and I would be very welcome to join her. She asks me whether I want the best for my family and my children, and where am I likely to find it. On one occasion on this farm we had a camp for 25 Palestinian children. I asked each one of them in turn what they wanted to do after they left school. Everyone, without exception, said that they wanted to leave the country. This is what the Israelis are hoping for. By making it as difficult as possible for us to continue living here, they hope that more and more of us will simply leave.

But, come what may, I am not going to leave: this is where I was born, and this is where I shall die, either of old-age or sickness, or perhaps sooner than I expect because of the violence meted out against us. I belong to this fourth group, and there are quite a lot of us. Here we are, and here will we stay!

There are also quite a number of Palestinians living in the 'corridor' between the 1949 armistice line (the de facto boundary between Israel and the West Bank) and where the Israelis have now constructed the Separation Barrier well to the east on Palestinian land. The official name for this corridor is 'the seam zone'. The thought is that these Palestinians will eventually get a special identity card (inevitably passing through checkpoints in the Barrier in order to go in and out) and those without this particular identity card will not be able to visit these communities. The Palestinian communities in the seam zone will find themselves increasingly isolated, living on the Israeli side of the barrier. I have little doubt that the Israeli hope is that this sense of isolation will also persuade a good number of them to leave this particular area and move to one of the Palestinian towns in the West Bank or to another country: simply another step in the increasing containment or removal of Palestinians. The comparison is often made between the policies of the Nationalist Party in South Africa during the apartheid years and the policies of the present Israeli regime. At that time in South Africa, the government there was creating isolated 'bantustans' for black Africans, and proposing that these bantustans could become separate black African states within South Africa. This is precisely the kind of practice that is being pursued in the West Bank, except that we Palestinians are having to live even more restricted lives than did the black

Africans of South Africa. For instance, here a completely separate network of roads is being built by the Israelis linking the illegal settlements from which Palestinians will be excluded. We will only be allowed to use the secondary roads, often quite narrow and poorly maintained, as I have said, making our journeys longer and potentially more dangerous.

# 8 MY FATHER'S HOPES, AND THE CIRCUMSTANCES THAT INFLUENCED THEM

Because I was only five years old when my father died, my memories of him are rather few, and I grew up not knowing a great deal about him.  But I gradually came to realise that he did have a real hope and vision for this piece of land which he, with the rest of my family, had inherited from his father.  It is this hope and vision that particularly my brother Daher and I are seeking to realise and carry forward.

My father's hope was undoubtedly earthed in his strong Christian conviction.  He read the Bible; he knew the Bible; he shared his understanding of the Bible with others, especially young people.  His hope and vision were also influenced by living under continuous occupation.  He was born under the Ottoman occupation of this country; he grew up under the British Mandate; he lived under Jordanian occupation; he died under the Israeli occupation.  From the day he was born until the day he died, this land was governed by others, part of someone else's territory, whether it was under the Ottoman Turks, the British rule, the Hashemite Kingdom of Jordan, or the State of Israel.

During the latter part of the Ottoman occupation, Christians were often persecuted and many left the country.  Christian emigration started that long ago, and has continued ever since.  When the British took over, Arab Palestinians were often treated very harshly, and there was the Arab revolt in 1936, which I have already mentioned in Note [2] on page 7, and which was put down ruthlessly and with many executions. The Arabs revolted against British rule because of our conviction that the British were favouring the Jews by turning a 'blind eye' to Jewish immigration in increasing numbers.

It is important to know that, in the years before the Jews declared the State of Israel in 1948, there were parts of this whole land where Jews and Arabs had for some while lived side-by-side in relative peace and harmony. This was particularly true before the Arab population began to feel itself threatened because of increasing Jewish immigration, and because the Jewish population was being given a greater say in the running of the country under the British Mandate. The Arab Palestinians were excluded from positions of power and influence under British rule because we had rejected the Balfour Declaration of 1917 [9] .

Jewish immigration was at first welcomed by the indigenous population of this country. Jewish people brought with them skills and knowledge that benefited this country. But what started benignly grew more and more into something to be feared in Arab eyes, because the local population began to feel that the increasing number of Jewish immigrants was bringing about a takeover of our land and resources.

I have mentioned that day in 1936 when my father and my uncle woke up one morning to discover that all our vines had been uprooted and destroyed overnight, and many other fruit trees as well. It was for my family our personal 'nakba' – catastrophe. My father and my uncle were faced with the need to begin all over again. Even in the years before 1948, the political situation was at times fraught and difficult. At that time there was an early Jewish settlement nearby called Kfar Etzion. Indeed, as early as 1927 there was a massacre in the settlement with Arabs killing a number of Jews. There are also stories of Palestinian families offering a safe refuge to Jews fleeing from the massacre. Tension increased between the incoming Jews and the indigenous Arabs in the 20s and 30s of the last century culminating, of course, in an outright war between the two communities following the declaration of the State of Israel in 1948. As is well known, this creation of the State of Israel was followed by an intense military campaign by the Jewish Haganah [10] that resulted over the next year or two in the destruction of 513 Palestinian villages and the creation of about 750,000 Palestinian refugees.

When the British withdrew from Palestine in 1948, handing back their Mandate to the new United Nations, they withdrew in a great hurry and did not leave behind them an ordered and structured administration for the land of Palestine [11]. Their departure created an administrative and military vacuum. Particularly during the latter years of the Mandate, the British had favoured the Jews over the Arabs, not least because the British refused to share administrative power with those who would not subscribe to the Balfour Declaration. We Arabs could not support the terms of the Balfour Declaration, and therefore were denied a proper share in the administration of this country compared with the Jews during the British Mandate. By 1948, the Jews in this land were therefore better organised, better armed, and better financed than the Arabs. They took full advantage of the political and military vacuum left by the British, and the rest – as we say – is history!

It was the declaration of the State of Israel that encouraged the indigenous Arab population of the country, whether Muslim or Christian, to talk about themselves as Palestinians. The Jews for their part more and more spoke of themselves as Israelis. But the words 'Palestine' and 'Palestinian' are not new words. This part of the world was called Palestine by the Romans. The Balfour Declaration itself talks about this land as Palestine. Before the State of Israel, all those living in this land saw themselves as Palestinians, so much so that the word itself was little used: there were the Jewish Palestinians; the Muslim Palestinians who were mostly Arab; and Christian Palestinians who were mostly Arab as well. So people here talked about themselves as Jews, Muslims or as Christians. And all of us Palestinians in that widest sense co-existed in this land, a land that was not a state or a nation, because it was continually under one sort of occupation or another: it was occupied territory. But once there was a self-declared State of Israel, then Arabs here became increasingly conscious of their Palestinian identity.

The Jordanians, among other Arab nations, came to the support of Arab Palestinians when war broke out in Palestine between Jews and Arabs following the British withdrawal. Jordanian troops occupied and defended that part of Palestine known now as the West Bank, and the armistice line endorsed by the United Nations in 1949 defines approximately the front lines at the time between Israeli forces and the Jordanian forces. From the date of the armistice until the Israelis overran and occupied the West Bank in 1967, the West Bank was under the administration of the Hashemite Kingdom of Jordan.

Prior to the British withdrawal in 1948, the United Nations had put forward a partition plan for the land of Palestine. (See [10] and second from left on the maps below.) This plan proposed allocating about 58% of the land to Jews and 42% of the land to the indigenous Arabs. However, at that time the Arab population comprised about 67% while the Jewish population was about 33%, and the Jews actually owned only about 6% of the land. The Jews welcomed the partition plan, but the Arabs rejected it because we thought it was unfair to our people. From our point of view, yet again the Jews were being favoured. In the light of history, if the Arabs had accepted that partition plan we would have saved ourselves a great deal of grief and tears. But history can never be written backwards, and it is completely understandable that at the time we Palestinians shouted, "No; unfair!"

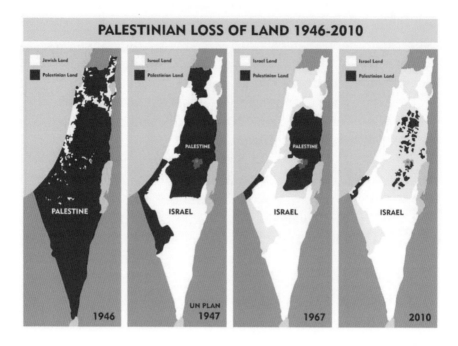

## PALESTINIAN LOSS OF LAND 1946-2010

This is the history that deeply affected my father. From his birth to his death this land was in one way or another a troubled land. His Christian conviction led him to say that this should not be so. It is not an exaggeration to say that he fashioned his life on the Beatitudes in the Gospel of Matthew. "Blessed are the peacemakers, for they shall be called children of God." He was convinced that Christians are called to be peacemakers, and his dream was to make possible different kinds of activities for children and young people on his farm through which they could learn the art of peacemaking. He and his family had been given this farm, this piece of land, by his father; and my father wanted to use it as a place of peacemaking. Sad to say, he died before his dream, his vision, could become a reality. The destruction of his farm in 1936 meant, of course, that he and his brother had to start again 'from scratch'. The produce from the farm was the only family income, so in the latter part of his life, inevitably, most of his energy went into recreating and tending his farm, in order to provide sufficiently for himself and his family.

My readers may well wonder how my brother and I have been able to take up and begin to realise my father's vision for this farm at a time when the political situation has significantly deteriorated since my father's own day. I have already written that, after school, I went to Austria to receive further education. I much enjoyed being in that country, and relishing the kind of freedom that Palestinians are not afforded in their own land. But something within me told me that I had to return, and I did so in June 1991. After the declaration by the authorities of our land as 'state land' a few months later, I began to see that it was no simple coincidence that I had felt his need to return: there was a purpose in it; indeed you might say that it was a calling. It was from that moment that my brother and I began to struggle to keep this farm which my grandfather had bought and also to seek to realise our father's vision. I felt that we should not simply do everything we could to hold on to it, but also enable it to become a place of positive peacemaking.

As I began to take forward both objectives, I did so with significant doubts and anxieties within my own mind and heart as to whether I was doing the right thing. And others, even some within my own family, suggested that I was attempting the impossible. For me, a significant moment was during the second intifada in 2000 when my family and I had to ask ourselves the question whether we were going to allow ourselves to remain in the chains of our recent history or whether we were going to break out and try something new. We chose the latter, and that was the start of what we now call 'The Tent of Nations' here at our farm.

It is not only the Israelis that have developed a 'victim mentality'. We Palestinians have done so as well. The Israeli victim mentality arises no doubt from the fact that they are hated in many parts of the Arab world because of the way they have snatched so much of Palestine from the indigenous population, and have been treating the population of the occupied territories so badly.

However, Israel is, and has been for some time, the most powerful nation in this part of the world, hugely supported by the United States, and a nuclear power as well. But the continuation of their myth of being the victim allows them to treat others in a way that no other modern democratic state would be allowed to do. The Palestinian 'victim mentality' arises from the fact that we are indeed in many ways weaker than the State of Israel: economically, militarily, and in terms of the quality of our leadership, and so on. But we use our evident weakness as an excuse to wait for others to act. We say that it is up to the powerful nations of the world to put pressure on Israel, and that meanwhile we can do nothing. My own thinking is that each one of us must take responsibility for the situation in which we find ourselves and act according to our ability. There is always *something* each one of us can do, and if each one of us did this, between us we could make the world of a difference. My time away from Palestine helped me greatly in this regard. It gave me a new self-confidence, and taught me the importance of taking the initiative, rather than sitting around and waiting for others to act.

So when I came back I suggested to my family and friends that in order to respond to the injustice that we and all Palestinians are suffering, we needed to create something positive on the farm. My spoken thoughts were sometimes met with puzzlement, and even ridicule. People wondered how we could develop anything really constructive and creative without a great deal of outside financial support. Any amount of obstacles were pointed out to me, over and over again. My own response was to establish some small projects, and to take care that they prospered, so as to give my critics something positive that they could see happening from which they could develop courage and hope.

My own family were largely supportive. My problem has been that I have had plenty of supporters, but fewer people who are prepared to come and take the initiative with me. Also, there have been three vital tasks that have needed our attention in parallel with one another: there is our vital presence on the land and the work on the farm, without which there would be no base for all else that we do. This is my brother's main responsibility, though of course he receives help from me and other members of the family and, more lately, volunteers who come and stay and work with my brother. Then there is the work of developing the vision, and this is my responsibility. Thirdly, there is the need to create and expand international awareness.

I find that maintaining and developing the vision can be quite difficult. It is easy to become distracted and discouraged. The current political climate does not help, because the road ahead sometimes seems to be blocked – both metaphorically and literally – whichever way I turn. Also, because we have been under Israeli occupation for so long, as a Palestinian people we have become reactive rather than proactive. That is very understandable, and I have no doubt that that is what the Israelis want. But it is not healthy for us, and I have made up my mind to be as proactive as possible, imagining new things to create and do, and trying my best to achieve them, despite all the obstacles.

After returning from Austria in 1991, one of my main objectives was to increase international awareness of the realities of the occupation. My time overseas gave me a greater international perspective, and also afforded me some useful contacts. My aim was to bring as many people as possible from overseas to visit the West Bank, and come and stay on our farm. At the time we had very little in the way of infrastructure to accommodate these visitors, but young people especially are able to cope for a short while with little in the way of domestic luxuries! So we encouraged people from overseas to come and plant olives and other fruit trees. When people started to arrive from abroad, this was a great encouragement to my family. "Hey! People care enough about us Palestinians to take the trouble to come and visit and see for themselves, and also offer practical help." Some of these internationals came specially to attend the court hearings when we were appealing against the declaration that our land was 'state land'.

We soon realised that there was the need to improve the infrastructure on the farm. It is by no means luxurious even now, not least because we are not allowed to build on the farm. This is a general rule in all parts of the West Bank under Israeli control (which is the majority). No construction by Palestinians is allowed since 1967 without a permit, but the granting of these permits rarely happens, and they are very expensive to obtain. Hence the fact that many Palestinians have in desperation built houses without a permit, and therefore illegally according to Israeli military law of the occupied territories. It is not that we have wanted to flout the law, merely that we need somewhere for our growing families to live, and permission to build simply cannot be obtained. Any building without a permit since 1967 is threatened with demolition. Over the years the Israelis have demolished over 55,000 Palestinian structures [12]. There are nine such demolition orders concerning our farm, which we are currently challenging in the courts.

So we were pressing ahead in two directions at the same time: challenging in the courts the proposed Israeli confiscation of our property, and at the same time improving the infrastructure to offer better accommodation to visitors. Some members of my family have been trying to persuade me to wait on the outcome of the legal battle before doing anything to improve the farm. My own feeling has been that we should not wait on the decision of the courts before pressing ahead with the improvements. Again, I felt the need to be proactive rather than simply waiting and seeing, which in Arabic we call 'inshAllah' – if God wills. I felt that God was willing me to move forward with the vision. The battle in the courts has already lasted 32 years with no clear outcome. To have sat around and done nothing to improve the farm for all that time would, I believe, have been a great mistake and not what

God would have wanted from us. It sometimes felt as if I was trying to drive a car forward with my foot on the accelerator while others were pulling hard on the handbrake and trying to make me stop! That is not to say that the use of the brake was not sometimes needed, because it stopped me from being too impulsive with my ideas.

I have made a list of things that I want to achieve, and from time to time jot down ideas that come into my head, realising that some of what I want is not achievable immediately, and must be a hope and objective for the future. I am also very conscious of the need to bring my family with me in my thinking and my hopes. I don't want to be the sort of person that just rushes on ahead, leaving everybody else behind. I want to create new opportunities in which other people can take a part, and within which other people can assume responsibility.

I have already said that most Palestinians react in one of three different ways to the present occupation: the way of violence; the way of resignation; or the way of flight. As I have indicated above, my family and I have chosen a fourth way: to stay put and resist the occupation through active, nonviolent resistance. And this is the way forward that a growing number of Palestinians are choosing.

**We who have chosen this path refuse to be anybody's enemies.** We will resist and overcome the evil within this situation, not with more evil, but with good. Rather than tell the other that he is wrong, we want to help the other discover by our loving actions that he is wrong. This is "to suffer the slings and arrows of outrageous fortune", but in a positive, proactive way; believing, as we do, that this military occupation cannot, and will not, last for ever, and that the State of Israel will either come to its senses of its own accord or be forced to do so by external circumstances which we cannot now predict, but we know from past history will one day happen. This is an essential part of our vision. We want

47

to build a bridge between land and people, and between people and people. We want to use our frustrations and disappointments constructively. **Frustrations and disappointments can give us the energy we need to do things positively, rather than become a seed-bed for anger and bitterness.**

The skill, and indeed the grace of God, is in discovering how to channel our pain into something constructive so that our situation, and indeed we ourselves, can be changed, in the hope that the situation of others, even those who oppose us, can also be changed. I am not thinking so much of bringing about political change, however necessary that is in the long-term, but of creating a climate for personal change, both in ourselves and others. The crucial question is, **How can I bring about a situation in which someone who has decided that I am his enemy can become my friend?**

On the farm we have made certain changes which can help us take forward the vision. One feature of our imposed isolation is that we have no mains water supply. So, we have dug new cisterns that catch and store rainwater, and this is what we use day by day. We have to be careful, but we have enough. We have no electricity supply, but some people in Germany have enabled us to have electricity generated by solar panels and stored in batteries. Not only has this overcome an injustice, but it is also an environmentally friendly way of producing electricity. Both the Israelis and we Palestinians claim to love this land, but neither community at times treats it with a great deal of love. For example, the Israelis greatly abuse its water supply, and degrade the environment by so doing; they build settlements – often ugly and aggressive looking – on the tops of beautiful hills; they pour vast amounts of concrete for their new roads, often spoiling the natural contours and creating ugly scars; the Separation Barrier itself is perhaps the most ugly wall in the world, and is very greedy of the land – usually Palestinian land – it consumes. We

Palestinians have also not yet learned a great deal about honouring our environment. We simply dump our garbage and building waste wherever convenient. If we go on like this, one day we might find that we are burying ourselves in our own garbage! At the Tent of Nations we want to set an example in terms of respect for the environment. The very fact that we are working our land and making it productive is a way of helping us and others reconnect with the land, which we Palestinians call 'our mother'.

It is also a fact that the non-governmental organisations, and there are very many in the West Bank and Gaza, are part of the problem as well as being part of the solution. Their presence, and the money they bring, and the people they employ help to create in us a spirit of dependency. We know that a great deal of foreign money, mainly American, is poured into the State of Israel (without which it would probably have to change radically tomorrow). But a lot of foreign money is also poured into the West Bank and Gaza, as if our problem was a humanitarian one. All this help is in danger of making us a nation of beggars. Our basic problem is not humanitarian, it is political: the fact of us having to live under occupation. The occupation has severely damaged our economy, which could in fact be thriving. We have the talents, we have the skills, we have or can acquire a lot of know-how. But trading, even among Palestinians living in different areas, has become increasingly difficult with all the restrictions. Exporting our products is often well nigh impossible.

Nevertheless, in spite of all these obstacles, we need to say both to ourselves and to others, "We are in charge of our own destiny". We have to decide what we want, and how others can help us achieve what we want. And then we can say to the outside world, "Here is where we intend to go; if you want to come with us and help us, you are welcome; if you want to dictate the terms, you are still our friends, but please don't tell us what to do!" An example of this was when some people from Germany came to the Tent of Nations and said to us, "How can we help?" You notice what they did not say: "This is what you ought to be doing next." We said to them that we would very much like to install a solar power system, and they agreed to help us. With solar power we have saved a considerable sum of money, not having to buy diesel fuel for electric generators. In addition, solar power is much more environmentally friendly than burning fossil fuel. This German support helped us to become more self-sufficient, which is one of our aims. We were most grateful for their involvement, because they worked with us in what we wanted to do, and what we would not have been able to achieve without their generous help. That is the right way forward: it is not one of dependence but of mutual cooperation and encouragement.

An Israeli Jew who stayed at the Tent of Nations returned a little while later and asked us what he could do to help us. "What are your own skills?" "Well, I am quite an expert at building compost toilets." "Marvellous," we said "just what we need!" And there they are, an essential part of our amenities, using no water and providing nutrition for fruit trees.

Compost toilets, using no water and providing nutrition for our crops

This kind of approach is also very helpful to people who visit Palestine. They often return home frustrated, aware of so many of the difficulties but feeling powerless about what they can do to change the situation. But every one of us, whoever we are, has the power and ability to make small changes. That is what those German people did by helping us; it has made a huge difference, and lasting difference. Things are better on the hill above the village of Nahalin because of their help and support. Yes, the overall political situation continues to deteriorate; the occupation is increasingly oppressive. But those who have worked with us have made a real difference, and so can everyone who wants to. We all have the power to "light a single candle rather than curse the darkness". I often use the example of a mosaic: such a picture is created with very small stones of different shapes and colours. Sometimes a bigger stone is needed, but for the most part the picture needs very small stones, each one of which, of itself, looks unimportant and insignificant. But each stone plays its own essential part in building up the whole illustration.

When we welcome people to the Tent of Nations, we want to offer them activities which will encourage them, and send them back to their own countries as people of hope, knowing that their own contribution, however small, has been a vital part in the whole mosaic of life. We want them to know that they can be peacemakers, first in their own community and family, but also peacemakers for the whole of this land in which Jews and Christians and Muslims are bound together in a common life, however separated from one another we seem to be at the moment.

*Notes:*

*[9] Lord Balfour, on behalf of the British Government of the time, promised a homeland in Palestine to Jewish people. As has been pointed out, this was a case of one nation [Britain] promising a second nation [the Jewish people] a homeland in the country of a third nation [the Arabs, Jews and Christians of Palestine], something which Britain had no right to do. Although the Declaration stated that "it being clearly understood that nothing shall be done which may prejudice the civil and*

*religious rights of existing non-Jewish communities in Palestine" that part of the Declaration was largely forgotten during the British Mandate of Palestine.*

*[10] An organization in what was then the British Mandate of Palestine from 1920 to 1948, which later became the core of the Israel Defence Force.*

*[11] The resolution noted Britain's planned termination of the British Mandate for Palestine and recommended the partition of the territory into two states, one Jewish and one Arab, with the Jerusalem-Bethlehem area being under special international protection, administered by the United Nations. The resolution included a highly detailed description of the recommended boundaries for each proposed state.*

*[12] The Israeli Committee Against House Demolitions estimates that, as of 2022, at least 55,048 houses have been demolished in the West Bank, East Jerusalem and Gaza since 1967, making perhaps as many as 100,000 people homeless: they are among the most recent Palestinian refugees.*

# 9 PLANTING A TREE AND MAKING A DIFFERENCE

The things we invite our visitors to become involved in are usually very simple, such as working on the land, planting trees and picking fruit, cleaning and preparing the soil; yes, and conversing with one another and sharing their hopes and fears.  There is also opportunity for Bible study and reflection.  We invite Israeli peace activists, Palestinians and internationals to come together and 'plant for peace'.

Planting a tree, you know, is for most people a very significant act.  Your hands are immersed deep in the soil of the land.  You handle carefully the young and tender roots that will soon push down through the soil that you have prepared so they can seek water and nourishment.  And it is only worth planting a tree if you have real hope for the future.  In your mind's eye you are seeing this tree in five or ten years' time, strong and healthy and bearing fruit year by year.  You are putting faith in the future, and in future generations, who will one day enjoy the fruit, quite literally, of your work.  One of the unkind things that Israeli settlers sometimes do is to invade a Palestinian farm and uproot the olive trees, particularly the ones newly planted.  That is what happened to us in 1936, but we do not know who the culprits were on that occasion.  Our response was not to give up on the future, but to plant new trees, even more than were planted before!  Far more olive trees have been planted here in Palestine than all the ones that have been uprooted by the Israeli state or by groups of settlers.  We are putting our faith in future generations, yes, future generations of Israelis as well, trusting that they, too, will come to their senses and that we can live together in this land in peace.

Not only is planting a tree a significant act of hope and trust in the future. It also shows respect for the environment: conserving and using the land for its fundamental purpose to "bring forth and multiply". Also it teaches us something important about true peace: that peace can only grow from the 'grass-roots' upwards. It can never be imposed from above. Politicians cannot bring about peace, though they do have their own part to play, not least as ordinary human beings. The handshake on the White House lawn of itself has not, and will never, bring about a true and lasting peace, or change anything fundamental. The change must come about in the hearts and minds of a sufficient number of ordinary people.

The act of planting a tree is also the giving and receiving of a gift. We give the gift of a young sapling to that part of the land; the land that will one day give us the fruit from the tree. We cannot give something that does not belong to us in the first place. Politicians often promise us things that they do not have of themselves and in themselves: that is why so many of their promises come to nothing. Often around us there is no peace, and perhaps there will be no peace for a long time. But if we have discovered a peace in our hearts, then we can be genuine peacemakers, fashioning here and there small areas of real peace, peace with justice; peace with respect; peace with a real love for one another. Significant change can come, even when the overall political situation remains unchanged.

On one occasion we had 25 students from Austria visit us. The day after they had departed, I had a telephone call from the leader of the group telling me how important for the students the visit to us had been. When I was talking to them, I had encouraged them not to make the problems that we are facing here in Palestine their chief concern. Much more important for them was to go back and become involved in issues of justice and peace in their own communities. The problem of Palestine is not the only problem in the world, nor the most intractable! Almost wherever we look we find situations of injustice and greed; yes, also in some of the most affluent and allegedly democratic countries in the world. Injustice is to be found on almost every doorstep. Their leader said to me that what we were doing at the Tent of Nations had given her students a new vision. They had seen the difference we were making to our situation in the small steps that we were taking; and they realised that they had the power to take similar small steps in their own communities that would also make a difference.

# 10 LEARNING FROM CHRIST

The land of Palestine was, of course, under a repressive occupation in Jesus' day. The Roman control of this land was no 'kid glove' affair. "Stick to what we tell you to do, and you will be all right. Step out of line, and oppose us in any way, and we will show you no mercy." That was the attitude of the occupying power then, and it is not dissimilar from our own situation. It was to those under occupation that Jesus spoke those profound words, "Blessed are those who know their need of God; blessed are those who hunger and thirst to see right prevail; blessed are the peacemakers ...." This is what he expected of those to whom he spoke; this is what he expects of us. No doubt many of his hearers were perplexed, saying among themselves, "How can we make peace; how can we see that right prevails?" But we can, starting with ourselves, in our own hearts and wills and lives. And until it starts there, we are unlikely to bring about true peace and justice anywhere else.

The Parable of the Talents [13] is a story told by Jesus from which I take much encouragement. You will remember that the master of the household gave ten talents to one servant, five talents to another, and one talent to a third. He then told them to make good use of what he had given them while he was away. On his return he called together his servants, asking them what they had done with the money he had handed to them on trust. The first two servants had used the money given to each of them wisely and were able to hand back to their master double what he had left with them. The third servant told his master that because he knew that his master was a hard man, someone whom he feared, he had simply hidden the talent he had been given, and done nothing with it, and was handing it back to his master. But the master condemned him, saying that the very least he could have done was to have invested the talent and gained some interest upon it, instead of just letting it lie idle while he was away. So too, I must not let the abilities that God has given me lie idle. I must use them in his service, thus increasing the value of them. The story also illustrates that each of us is given different gifts. The quality and quantity of the gifts are not for us to choose. However, the way we put them to use is for each one of us to choose.

This parable is very much in my mind when we gather children together at the Tent of Nations for a summer camp. In July each year we invite children from the Bethlehem area and surrounding districts to come and camp on our hilltop farm for a few days. And children do come, not just from the wealthier backgrounds. We have young people from the refugee camps and children from poor families. What we encourage them to do while they are with us is to discover their God-given talents, whatever these may be, and start to use them. On one occasion we invited the children to write a story about whatever they chose. We gathered these stories together and put them in a book. When parents came to collect their children, we read out some of these stories, and then told them who had written each story. Some of the parents of the storytellers were very surprised to hear such a story read out that had been written by their own child. "We simply didn't realise that he or she had this kind of talent!" they told me. The prevailing Palestinian culture of parent towards child is still a very protective one. The majority of children are not encouraged to be adventurous. "Don't go looking for opportunities; inshAllah they will come to you." But that is not the way it happens, and I want our next generation of young people to be much more adventurous, much more inquisitive, and much more daring with their lives.

*Notes:*

*[13] Matthew 25:14-30; Luke 19:12-28*

# 11 OUR VISION

In Chapter 8, writing about my father's hopes for this farm, I have already shared with you a great deal about our own hopes and vision for this place which we have inherited from him.

Our 'creed' - we refuse to be anybody's enemy !

My brother and I want the Tent of Nations to grow as a place where people from near and far can come and see for themselves, be educated and informed and, above all, go away with a new sense of empowerment and hope. I already see this happening in the faces and remarks of some of those who have visited us. When I tell and retell our story, a story of apparent hopelessness is turned into a 'lighted candle' of hope because other people can learn from us that, whatever the difficulties and disappointments that we all experience, there is always something that we can do to challenge and improve the situation.

Except when prevented by the Covid epidemic, every year I travel abroad usually twice to the United States and once to Europe, at the invitation of Friends of the Tent of Nations, to give talks in churches and other gatherings, where again I simply tell our story. These visits abroad also give me the opportunity of meeting some people in positions of power and influence, who are often largely unaware of the 'situation on the ground' here in Palestine. I am convinced our story remains a story of hope, not of despair, and this can and does inspire hope in others not just for us here in Palestine but in their dealings with their own problems, conflicts and disappointments. In this sense, our vision is that this farm is not just a plot of agricultural land but almost a sacred place, proclaiming a beacon of hope in a world where there is too much darkness.

Our tools for this are very simple:
- Trust in God for whom, I really do believe, nothing in heaven or on earth is totally hopeless. There is always something we can do with His help.
- Daher's and my family who are of tremendous support and encouragement to us.
- Our many international friends throughout the world whose support and timely interventions have helped us to survive and persevere.

We encourage all who can to 'Come and See'. In addition to the camps for children, we also run work camps for adults who come and help us on the farm; we gather people together for the olive and the almond harvest, and for the grape harvest. Those who come might be asked to renovate a cave in June, plant some trees in April, or harvest olives in October. But, whatever, we come together in the morning and share in the work that is needed. In the afternoons we have an educational programme, sometimes with field trips.  Later, after the evening meal, we focus on cultural activities: we gather round the fire and perhaps we sing together or someone recites some poetry or tells a story or plays an instrument.  Here again, it is the local Palestinians that need the most encouragement.  The 'victim' mentality which has so bedevilled our lives means that the idea of voluntary work does not come naturally to us.  The internationals who come and live among us are the 'volunteers'.  The thought of ourselves being 'volunteers' has still to take root in our society.  I heard about a tree-planting project in a nearby village recently when a number of internationals had gathered to help with the planting, along with quite a large group of young Palestinian teenagers.  The actual work of tree planting was done mostly by the internationals and older Palestinian men and women; our young lads seemed quite happy to walk about waving Palestinian flags and chanting freedom songs; they actually did very little of the work that was needed!

We Palestinians are very good at telling others, particularly visitors from other countries, our sad stories.  And we certainly have plenty to tell.  But when it comes to doing something to correct the situation, we too often wait to be told by others rather than taking the responsibility into our own hands.  It is this kind of attitude that I want to help change in our work at the Tent of Nations.  I hope that that we can move to a situation where our schools, right from the first grade, encourage our children to take on voluntary work of some kind.  Schools could easily begin to organise this, and it could become part of our national life.  We do not have an army in which to serve, unlike Jewish children who have to do two or three years of military service (not that I'm suggesting that this does them much good!).  Wouldn't it be marvellous if we were to create our own national *voluntary* service, which will educate our young people to take responsibility, to feel connected to their society, and to be of practical help to other people?

Among those who come to our camps are some young Jewish people. They don't come in large numbers, but some do come and share our life and discover how we Palestinians live. And I have to say that their eyes are usually opened. They say to me, "We did not know it was like this." "Well, now you do know," I tell them, "and it is your responsibility to go back to your homes and do whatever you can within your own capability. If you go back and forget all about us, you will not only be betraying us; you will be betraying yourselves by denying your own ability to bring about some kind of change, however small." A number of Jews (I say Jews rather than Israelis, because of course there are about two million Palestinian Israelis) who have visited us return a second time, no doubt to reinforce their own commitment for change and out of real concern for our predicament.

So my hope is that our farm, which we call the Tent of Nations, will grow into a small school of hope and empowerment where we help people to learn how to change, principally to change themselves so that they may bring about a change in others and eventually in society. We don't belong to ourselves; we belong to one another. I am told that Africans have a marvellous word for this, which is 'ubuntu': it means I am what I am because of who we all are. The Palestinians and the Israelis have yet to understand the true meaning of that word, to take it to their hearts, and to live it out in their lives.

# ABOUT THE AUTHOR

Daoud Nassar is a native of Bethlehem, Palestine. He is married to Jihan, and they have three children in their family. Daoud is a Lutheran Christian, fluent in Arabic, German and English, with a Degree in Biblical Studies from a Bible School in Austria, a BA Degree in Business from Bethlehem University, and a Degree in Tourism Management from Bielefeld University in Germany. He manages the farm known as Daher's Vineyard located in the West Bank of Palestine and directs the work of the programmes and projects known as the **Tent of Nations**.

Annually, nearly 7,000 international tourists visit the Nassar family's ancestral land – a 100-acre hilltop site situated between Bethlehem and Hebron in the West Bank. The attraction is the **Tent of Nations**, an open and free enclave that serves as an educational and cultural centre for local Palestinians and Israelis, including the international visitors.

The Nassar family land, purchased in 1916 by Daoud Nassar's grandfather, is surrounded by Jewish settlements on three sides and the Palestinian village of Nahalin on the fourth. The land is cut off from sources of water and electricity, and the family is resisting the loss of their land by going through the courts with proof of ownership and by employing non-violent responses to Israeli laws that limit growth and personal freedom. Activities such as planting olive trees, developing alternative energy sources, and improving ways to collect, store and use water supplies wisely are just some of the ways in which the Nassars fight for human dignity.

The **Tent of Nations** also offers summer camps for Arab youth so that through shared activities they may learn about one another. Women from Nahalin are enrolled throughout the year at the Women's Education Center in courses such as English, Computer Science, Management, Accounting and Creative Writing. Students at Bethlehem University have the opportunity to perform service projects on the land itself as a part of their degree studies. Through the **Tent of Nations**, Daoud works each day to prepare the people on the land for the day when the walls come down.

Printed in Great Britain
by Amazon